CHA
Collective Healing Anonymous Basics

Published by Collective Healing Anonymous

Copyright © 2024 Collective Healing Anonymous

All rights reserved.

ISBN: 978-0-9862276-3-9

All images and pictures are used in compliance with the sources content license agreement.

CHA

Collective Healing Anonymous Basics

Empowering Non-Religious Spirituality toward Self-Discovery, Healing, Feeling, and Awakening, Together!

Table of Contents

- 2 — About CHA
- 3 — What's Happening to Us?
- 5 — Welcome to Your Empowerment Process
- 7 — Amazing Evolution of 12-Step Programs
- 11 — Why Collective Healing Anonymous?
- 13 — Foundational Themes of CHA
- 15 — From Surviving to Thriving - Understanding the CHA Vision
- 16 — Empowering Clients Beyond the Office - A Special Note to Mental Health Professionals
- 17 — Changing the Narrative of Addiction and Dependency
- 18 — The Power of Sacred Processes Like Meditation, Yoga, and Self Inquiry
- 19 — Trust the Process

Getting Started in CHA 20

- 20 — Getting Started in CHA
- 21 — The Official 12 Steps
- 23 — A Deeper Look into CHA
- 27 — The Four Pillars of CHA
- 28 — Meditation Basics
- 29 — Yoga Basics
- 30 — Self-Inquiry Basics

Your CHA Tool Box 32

- 32 — Suggested Books by Category
- 33 — Online Resources & Guiding Principles
- 34 — How to Conduct a Basic CHA Meeting?
- 37 — How to Start a CHA Support Group?
- 38 — 30-Day Life-Principles Practice
- 40 — Appreciating Now
- 42 — Dear Friends

ABOUT CHA

Collective Healing Anonymous (CHA) emerges as a groundbreaking non-religious process and support group that transcends the limitations of traditional 12-step programs, offering a fresh perspective rooted in collective consciousness and deep introspection toward Self-Discovery, Healing, and everlasting Inner Freedom. CHA further provides the absolute potential to fully recover from any and all obsessions, compulsions, addictions, dependencies, and identity matters, in THIS LIFE!

In short, Collective Healing Anonymous is a Revolutionary and Empowering Possibility to heal, feel, and awaken, together! This book, *CHA Basics*, in simple and relatable terms, shares CHA's foundational purpose, basic structure, and essential ingredients for fully understanding and participating in the CHA Process and Community. This guide also shares compassionate wisdom and guidance toward healing and awakening, what to expect when attending meetings, and the importance of including Sacred Processes in your life, as well as providing specific and easy to follow tips to begin living the life you know in your heart is possible. Lastly, detailed instructions about how to start and conduct a CHA gathering in your area are available in the Tool Box Section of this book.

Moving forward, to allow Collective Healing Anonymous to best work for you, it may be helpful to understand that CHA is not a belief system, philosophy, and not a religious teaching; does not ascribe to any single doctrine, guru, or spiritual master. It is, however, a supportive non-religious spiritual process and support system focused on collective healing through inner transformation and personal growth, using a variety of resources, even science; and focusing on CHA's official 12 steps to liberation.

> "IT IS TIME TO GIVE OURSELVES A LOVING BREAK FROM FIGHTING WITH ONE ANOTHER AND JUDGING OURSELVES, BY HEALING, FEELING, AND AWAKENING, TOGETHER.

Another highly relevant consideration is this: CHA can be used as a companion to any 12-step or non 12-step program, healing and awakening modality like yoga, or counseling process you may be utilizing. Unlike programs that demand exclusivity, CHA embraces absolute inclusivity, recognizing that healing and growth can come from a variety of sources. This flexibility allows individuals to integrate the CHA process with their existing practices without conflict, enhancing their overall journey; which easily supports and complements other methods by offering an additional layer of depth and understanding. By not mandating exclusivity, and also providing the option to establish your own steps, CHA empowers individuals to create a personalized and holistic trajectory to their healing and awakening. This approach naturally nurtures a more comprehensive and fulfilling path to self-discovery, while connecting with a community of like-minded friends steeped in collective wisdom. Other available resources, references and literature may be found at the CHA's official website: www.DiscoverCHA.org.

What is Happening to Us?

> It is time for us to compassionately remove our innocent masks and free ourselves! "

We are witnessing the flowering of human consciousness.

We are all born into this wildly amazing and beautiful world filled with mystery, paradox, and awe, harnessing the life-liberating capacity to consciously engage in thinking for ourselves. Around the age of two, most everyone begins to discover this profound ability. However, what soon follows is the creation of a cocoon around us by those who raise us—parents, societies, religious and governmental authorities, teachers, and conditioned group opinions. These forces influence us to think the way 'they' do, to feel, imagine, behave, identify, and believe as 'them.' We are taught to deny our inner sacred wisdom, our natural curiosity, and effortless expressions, and instead, we are molded into something we are not. This cocoon turns us away from the Universal Intuition within ourselves.

Universal Intuition is a wisdom and conscious clarity that transcends living from the conflicted perspective of self-preservation and the divisive forces of survival mode. Thus, we have temporarily lost our conscious tenacity to genuinely think for ourselves free from our programming, conditioned biases, and the limitations of survival instincts.

To emerge from this cocoon, we must reclaim our mental powers to question our beliefs and motivations deeply, compassionately, and honestly. This inner investigation and awakening will help us break free from our unconscious, self-defeating, and innocently destructive habits, both individually and collectively as humanity. In this earnest and honest process of healing, feeling, and awakening, we naturally regain autonomy over our bodies and minds. We must awaken from our trance, from our innocent delusions, denial, and self-neglect; which means calling attention to our essential, peaceful, and joyous being already here, now, within us—already whole, complete, enough! We must allow ourselves to individually and collectively heal, starting with embracing our primal innocence and having tender mercy for ourselves. It is time.

The Crossroads, Conscious Decision, and Commitment

Regarding finding true happiness, when the guarantees offered by parents, teachers, governing and religious leaders, doctors, therapists, and culture prove unreliable, untrustworthy, and untrue—empty promises of finding security and everlasting fulfillment outside of ourselves or even salvation after death—we come to a crossroads. To continue choosing the same unconscious and painful path of confusion and division - OR - consciously choose to genuinely heal, feel, and awaken, now, permanently and honestly—True Freedom!

The decision point is this: To either question our rigid belief systems deeply and sincerely - OR - choose to believe more unreliable versions of a promised dream sold through the pursuit of conditional happiness—ideas that cannot possibly work for everyone, or anyone actually.

When we observe society and the world, this becomes evident: We spend most of our lives trying to find the "Promise" of a fulfilling existence through what we have been taught to believe is true and reliable about life, others, and ourselves. And when those ideas never turn out to be as promised, we default to coping mechanisms and survival strategies to deal with our hurt and inner conflict. That is to say, we begin relying on our addictions, compulsions, and obsessions for a fleeting sense of relief which intensifies our anxiety, stress, and pangs of unworthiness; rather than seeking our true source of happiness within.

We grapple with self-criticism, blame, self-judgment, guilt, and shame, living lives of quiet desperation, lost in our obsessions and compulsions, and mostly unaware of the profound depths of our unconscious, painful, and divisive habits no longer serving us. We even judge our judging and remain unaware of that self-defeating loop by allowing the mind to beat itself up through thought. And when our coping habits stop providing the relief to which we have become attached, to cope with yet another round of inner conflict, many find themselves further entangled in self-sabotaging routines like blame and finger-pointing. No wonder many of us opt into a wild array of coping mechanisms as dependencies and addictions to innocently find a semblance of peace and relief. No wonder why some of us even fall victim to the belief that there is no way out other than suicide, although a permanent solution to an absolutely temporary condition.

The Heart of the Matter - There is Always Good News!

At the heart of our apparent suffering is this: We are unaware that the majority of what we believe and identify with is not the reality of ourselves, and it causes great pain, worry, fear, unworthiness, self-judgment, contempt, and self-punishment. All of this inner suffering indicates we are temporarily lost in the prison of our minds which our deeper intuition constantly grapples with—minds filled primarily with socially acceptable, self-defeating ideas no longer serving us. It seems like there are always conflicting thoughts like "Should I do this or should I do that?" dominating the mind and running our lives, as well as identifying with untrue rationalizations such as, "I shouldn't be feeling this way" or "I'm not good enough." However, amid whatever we are struggling with there is always good news when we open our hearts and minds.

When we allow ourselves to become open and willing to have the experience we are having, and feel what we are feeling right here now, we begin to notice a deeper intelligence within us—a deeper wisdom that knows something just isn't right with our current perceptions of ourselves, others, life, the world, and reality. Something knows that continuing to believe the endless mental chatter of the mind to find a complete and peaceful sense of self is not working, and never has. We are becoming aware that continuing to look outside of ourselves or to the mind's programming we received from external sources—to provide us with a sense of self, clarity, meaning, and purpose—will never fully heal or liberate us; because it never has and never will.

Oh...What to do?

There is GOOD NEWS! There are options! There is inspiration! There is a power greater than hope within yourself yearning to be revealed! The Real YOU! And there is help. There is another way to be...alive!

Welcome to Your Empowerment Process!

Dear Friends,

In a world where suffering often feels like the norm as individuals continue struggling with addictions, obsessions, and compulsions, and identity crises are on the rise, a profound evolution is underway. Welcome to Collective Healing Anonymous (CHA)! Welcome to your Empowerment Process! Welcome to genuine Self-Discovery!

Although the potential to heal and liberate yourself from any and all dependency matters and identity challenges is available through the 12-Step CHA Process, it is important to recognize that genuine Self-Discovery is our primary spiritual aim, as we reclaim autonomy and power over our bodies and minds; with recovery from addiction, obsessions, and compulsions being a natural byproduct of your healing, feeling, and awakening journey.

CHA is also quite different from other traditional Programs in three distinct ways: Most recovery-based processes often emphasize powerlessness. CHA's approach, however, is about reclaiming our natural power over the mind— to use the mind instead of continuing to allow the mind to work on it's own behalf (ego).

Secondly, other programs often claim that addiction and dependency are lifelong afflictions and identities, notions that CHA categorically rejects. CHA recognizes that what we refer to as addictions and dependencies - OR - obsessions and compulsions are merely temporary coping mechanisms that one can be absolutely free of IN THIS LIFE!

And thirdly, CHA is not a belief system and does not attempt to make you believe in any doctrine, philosophy, or teaching. It is completely up to you to discover what works for you, and what does not; and, what is true for you in this moment, or not. YOU have the power of choice. And, reclaiming that superpower as well as various others you may be unaware of is an enormous part of CHA'a Step One.

We understand that you are not alone; that everyone is temporarily suffering from various types of obsessions, identity challenges, coping mechanisms, cultural conditioning, family programming, or addictions; and that this program is not for those who need it, but for those who freely choose it. Welcome to Empowerment and Self-Liberation! Welcome to Healing, Feeling, and Awakening!

Welcome to Collective Healing Anonymous - CHA!

Allowing Compassionate COURAGE

Obsessions, compulsions, addictions, and identity struggles naturally fall away as we allow compassionate courage and loving acknowledgement to heal the pain and unattended sorrow that fuels them.

THE AMAZING EVOLUTION
OF 12-STEP PROGRAMS

If you identify as a Human Being then you most likely have heard of Alcoholics Anonymous (A.A.) or at least the concept of alcoholism. But did you know that in 1934, in Akron, Ohio, A.A. became the Mother of the original 12-step program? Designed to help individuals recover from alcoholism through a structured process of personal and spiritual development, these programs have since given birth to several other recovery initiatives worldwide. Today, it is estimated that there are over 123,000 A.A. groups globally, positively impacting millions of lives. Moreover, the offspring of A.A., such as Overeaters Anonymous, Al-Anon, ACOA, Narcotics Anonymous, Sex Addicts Anonymous, Gamblers Anonymous, and many others have led to the formation of over half a million 12-step support groups worldwide.

But why is there a new 12-step program called Collective Healing Anonymous when so many options already exist? To understand this, let's delve into the history, claims, and some misconceptions about A.A. and the 12 Steps.

The Foundations and Misconceptions of A.A.

Contrary to popular belief, A.A. and 12-step programs are not fundamentally addiction recovery programs, and remarkably so, no where do the 12 steps mention alcoholism or adopting a personal identity as an "alcoholic" as part of the process; which implies the true potential of all 12-step programs is to free ourselves from self-victimizing, self-judging, and limiting personal identities. At its core, the 12-step process is designed to help individuals awaken to the universal truth of themselves. In fact, recovery from addiction is actually the byproduct of healing, feeling, and awakening through any traditional 12-step process.

While A.A. primarily focuses on alcohol addiction recovery, for example, the principles of A.A. can benefit anyone seeking a freer life and higher purpose. The underlying message in A.A.'s literature and meetings is that adherence to their basic set of spiritual principles (the 12 Steps) can transform lives and solve all of your problems. These ideas are at the heart of most recovery programs using A.A.'s traditional 12 steps; like those groups mentioned above.

Furthermore, A.A. literature states that the fundamental problem for alcoholics is a spiritual malady, not specifically alcohol overconsumption; and that the primary cause of their issues lie in an obsessive mind, not merely substance abuse. A.A. claims that there is a spiritual solution to every problem, again suggesting anyone can benefit spiritually from working the steps. For instance, the A.A. 12 Steps and 12 Traditions book reports, "Growing spiritually is the answer to our problems." These amazing promises offered through the traditional 12 Steps have been adopted by millions, clearly indicating there are healing and liberating forces operating beyond the human intellect; forces that anyone can somehow awaken to; similar to classical understandings and interpretations of Enlightenment or Self-Realization.

This wildly fascinating claim—that there is a spiritual solution to all of one's problems—suggests there is a deeper universal possibility that absolutely transcends limited human perspectives—perspectives beyond the limitations and filters of one's conditioned mind. And at the deepest level, suggests there exists a possibility to be completely free of our primal addiction to self-preservation and survival mode; possibilities to be liberated from all suffering in this life; that is, when we no longer allow the "personal will" (Psychological Self/Ego) to run our lives, but turn it over to the Universe, God, Reality, Cosmic Consciousness. A trancendent and Divine option not limited to "Alcoholics" but everyone!

The Deeper Truths of A.A.

Specifically, A.A.'s foundational guide called the Big Book, on page 42, speaks of the possibility of total liberation and inner freedom based upon this realization by one of its founding members, "Quite as important was the discovery that spiritual principles would solve all my problems." Tens of thousands have discovered the life-liberating truths of A.A.'s universal principles, experiencing benefits far beyond mere addiction recovery. For a relatively small number of participants who genuinely, willingly, and wholeheartedly trust the program's guidance, this unwritten message is clear: "A.A. is a Spiritual Program." And despite that the 12 steps can be written on a half sheet of paper, and are in essence the entire healing and awakening spiritual process itself, nothing more, nothing less, and that anyone can follow them, only a handful among millions of participants ever fully surrender to the simplicity of the universal principles embedded in them.

Challenges and Barriers

There are numerous options for anyone ready to heal, feel, and awaken from a life dominated by the obsessive and compulsive nature of the egoic mind. Virtual 12-Step meetings accessible at all hours through mobile phones make it even easier. However, this raises an important question: "Why do the majority of people suffering from their unconscious, obsessive, and compulsive minds avoid 12-step support despite the abundance of healing and awakening possibilities?"

The answer is straightforward. It appears that approximately 97 percent of people offered 12-step programs turn away from them due to two main reasons: religious undertones and the concept of powerlessness. Specifically, the use of the word "God" and the idea of surrendering one's personal power to one's concept of God are significant deterrents.

While it is widely understood that our personal will or egoic nature often interferes with our inherent joy, ease, and appreciation for life, many people are unaware that religion has been a tool for the egoic mind to corrupt, abuse, and misinform. Consequently, any use of religious language in support groups often repels rather than attracts. Regardless of individual religious or non-religious beliefs, there is often an unconscious mistrust of programs using traditional religious language. For example, the word "God" appears four times in the original 12 steps, which alienates many potential participants. Ironically, many people have chosen to attend "recovering from religion" support groups before considering traditional 12-step recovery, or even returning to their faith.

Collective Healing Anonymous addresses these issues by using the most inclusive language and unifying concepts possible and states, "All that CHA offers are merely suggestions, not rigid rules."

Moreover, historically, for thousands of years, people have turned to religion for help, only to feel let down, abused, or disappointed. They often find that the same ego-driven energies they seek to escape are prevalent within religious institutions. This underlying mistrust of most religions, along with their divisive and forceful actions and language, explains why so many avoid traditional 12-step programs which often confuse religion with true spirituality.

The Difference Between Religion and True Spirituality

Religion and true spirituality, while often intertwined, are fundamentally different in essence and practice. Religion typically involves organized and rigid beliefs, rituals, and dogmas associated with a specific faith community, often emphasizing adherence to established doctrines and external practices. It often becomes lost in the idea, "Believe us, not them, because we have the answers," which always leads to inner conflict and external divisions. In contrast, true spirituality is a personal and individual journey that transcends specific doctrines, beliefs, and rituals. It emphasizes inner growth, self-awareness, and a direct connection with the divine or higher consciousness through any variety of resources and guidance. True spirituality seeks universal truths and personal enlightenment beyond the limitations of rigid beliefs, promoting inclusivity, compassion, and inner peace from the source already within you. Unlike religion, which is always influenced by cultural and historical contexts, true spirituality is always here now, as a universal pursuit of deeper meaning, authentic Self-Discovery, and Enlightenment beyond the confines of organized belief systems and group identities.

Evolving 12-Step Programs

Human consciousness is evolving, and so must our approaches to healing, feeling, and awakening. The phrase "I am spiritual but not religious" is becoming more popular among those genuinely interested in consciously participating in their own evolution; and reflects a growing distinction between religion and true spirituality. Similar to Collective Healing Anonymous (CHA) are movements like Science and Nonduality (SAND) for example, that explore the intersection of science and spirituality, highlighting the need for healing processes that empower individuals without religious or cultural constraints. Furthermore, the healing and awakening possibilities of Yoga are becoming more popular through options like Y12SR, which stands for "Yoga of 12-Step Recovery." It is a holistic approach that integrates the wisdom of yoga with the practical tools of 12-step programs.

    The time has come to officially accept the evolution of the original 12-step process into something more reflective of our contemporary world. This shift involves moving away from religious language and concepts toward a universal spirituality that also includes scientific perspectives, while not dismissing the universal principles inherent in all of the world's religions. Healing and waking up to the truth of us is about embracing our inherent power and opening ourselves to a universal trust beyond the limitations of the egoic mind.

Collective Healing Anonymous

As we recognize and honor the progress made by the original 12-step programs and grace of consciously evolving through the challenges of religion, we welcome the new era of Collective Healing Anonymous (CHA). This revolutionary 12-step process aligns with our current state of human consciousness, offering more inclusive language and concepts that move us beyond divisive and ego-driven approaches. CHA aims to provide spiritual, practical, and scientific guidance and solutions that transcend the limitations of traditional 12-step programs, opening new possibilities for self-discovery, healing, and awakening in a collective and all-inclusive manner.

    Let us compassionately let go of what no longer serves us and willingly open our hearts and minds to embrace fresh, new 12-step guidance towards genuine self-discovery, healing, and collective awakening, together!

GRATITUDE

Who is Collective Healing Anonymous for?

Collective Healing Anonymous is for anyone and everyone seeking a more conscious way to be happy, joyous, and free! A more pleasant and unifying way to be alive and peacefully coexist beyond life-restricting obsessions, compulsions, addictions, and divisive beliefs, identities, and habits.

WHY CHA?

What CHA Offers...

- Connecting with like-minded friends interested in healing, feeling, and awakening, together and individually.
- Engaging with and participating in non-religious, yet spiritual and non-judgmental support group gatherings.
- Self-Discovery toward Peaceful Coexistence and Self-Realization, Enlightenment.
- Potential to heal from all obsessions, compulsions, addictions, and identity crises, IN THIS LIFE!
- Growing up and waking up as mature and unconditionally loving human beings; and understanding the many gifts of Sacred Processes.
- Learning from the collective wisdom of the CHA community.
- Support, wisdom, and guidance for physical, mental, emotional, and spiritual well-being; and more!

www.discoverCHA.org

YES! THERE IS ANOTHER WAY TO BE ALIVE!

Embracing your primal
INNOCENCE

You are innocent, worthy, and deserving, already, always. Do not believe the mind or anyone that says anything in opposition to this sacred reality. Embracing primal innocence empowers us, freeing the mind from self-hate, unworthiness, criticism, and blame. True Healing.

Foundational Themes of Collective Healing Anonymous

It's Okay
This reassures you that whatever you're feeling or going through is acceptable and neither makes you a good nor bad person. "It's okay" is an acknowledgement that everyone faces challenges, and it's perfectly natural to seek out help and humbly receive support, unconditionally.

You are not Alone
This reminds you there are others who have experienced similar struggles, and somehow opens the door to dissolving the idea of disconnection holding us back from coming out of our shell and truly blossoming.

We are Here for You
This underscores the healing power of a support system. It means that there are people who will not judge or condemn you, who genuinely care about your well-being, and are unconditionally willing to assist you on your journey. You do not have to face your struggles in isolation.

There is Another Way to Be Alive
This offers inspirational and life-liberating energy and possibility there are alternative paths to living a fulfilling and meaningful life beyond our habits, routines, and beliefs no longer serving us. It encourages you to explore new possibilities and creativity beyond your current struggles.

You Have Choices
This empowers you by reminding us that we have the agency and power to make decisions about our lives. You wield the power of choice to consciously choose healthier and more constructive paths; recognizing you are NOT bound by your past choices, beliefs, feelings, and behaviors.

You Are Allowed
This is about giving ourselves permission to think, feel, and express ourselves beyond our critical inner voices. We are allowed to have the experience we are having right here now, without trying to mentally change it or judge it. You are allowed to be exactly as you already are. Perfectly whole.

You are Already Whole, Worthy, Innocent, Complete, Enough
This highlights your everlasting, natural, and intrinsic innocence, worthiness and completeness. It signifies that you do not need external validation or to modify your behavior or use substances to feel whole. You are already complete, loveable, enough, just as you are; always! Even when acting out addictions.

Opening to infinite

ABUNDANCE

Say and repeat this: I am not the body; I am not even the mind. I am infinite abundance, limitless possibilities, pure loving potential, unconditional love. I am life itSELF; free to be free or free to be bound.

UNDERSTANDING THE COLLECTIVE HEALING ANONYMOUS VISION

EXPANDING YOUR POSSIBILITIES

From Surviving to Thriving

Participating in a group environment within Collective Healing Anonymous (CHA) holds profound significance as it symbolizes the act of "coming out of hiding" from the shackles of shame, fear, unworthiness, and guilt that bind us. Within an environment of emotional security free of judgment, wrapped in the arms of acceptance of the CHA community, we have the opportunity to openly share our experiences, vulnerabilities, insights, and collective wisdom. This act of sharing is an essential step towards breaking free from the isolation and fear that often accompanies addiction, dependency issues, and identity challenges.

In the loving and gentle embrace of the CHA community, we find the compassionate courage and strength to shed the layers of shame and secrecy that have held us captive. We emerge from hiding, empowered and harmonious, allowing our authentic selves to shine forth, thereby reclaiming our inherent autonomy over our minds and bodies. This collective journey transcends dependency and addiction matters, obsessions and compulsions, and identity crises, thereby fostering deep healing, ultimately leading to the awakening of a more genuine, liberated, and complete sense of self.

Empowering Clients Beyond the Office: The CHA Option

A Special Note to Mental Health Professionals

Collective Healing Anonymous (CHA) emerges as a groundbreaking non-religious process and support group option that transcends the limitations of traditional 12-step programs, offering a fresh perspective rooted in collective consciousness and deep introspection toward Self-Discovery, Healing, Inner Freedom, and the potential to fully recover from any and all obsessions, compulsions, addictions, dependencies, and identity matters, in this LIFE!

Collective Healing Anonymous (CHA) recognizes that clients need more than just weekly counseling sessions. They require a loving, supportive community focused on feeling, healing, and awakening. CHA addresses the gap in client care by providing continuous support beyond the office. Our community-driven approach ensures that clients are not completely left to their own devices outside of the clinical setting, fostering ongoing connection and growth. By integrating holistic practices and peer support, CHA empowers individuals to thrive, offering a nurturing environment where true healing extends beyond traditional therapy. Join us in transforming client care through compassionate, continuous support, beyond the office. www.DiscoverCHA.org

CHA is a Wonderful & Loving Support Group.

UNDERSTANDING THE COLLECTIVE HEALING ANONYMOUS VISION

WRITE YOUR OWN STORY

Changing the Narrative of Addiction & Dependency

In Collective Healing Anonymous (CHA), we recognize that dependency and addiction matters have long been stigmatized and misunderstood. We believe it is time to shift the conversation and reframe those ideas to what they truly are—temporary coping mechanism dependencies that you can absolutely be freed from in this life! In other words, CHA accepts that dependencies are NOT life long afflictions but opportunities to learn and grow; to feel, heal, and awaken! By acknowledging that all dependency issues, compulsions, obsessions, and identity challenges, whether they manifest as substance abuse or compulsive behaviors, which are rooted in the innocent human drive for temporary relief from inner pain and discomfort, we remove a tremendous amount of guilt, fear, judgment, and shame, often associated with those life-restricting survival and coping strategies.

Furthermore, the CHA approach and understanding of healing and awakening recognizes that we innocently turn to coping mechanisms and survival strategies as a way to navigate our emotional and psychological challenges, and existential concerns. By shifting the traditional understanding, language, and perspective to one of innocence, empowerment, and compassionate understanding, we more openly and willingly embrace the possibility of absolute healing and liberation from all obsessions, compulsions, identity crises, and addiction matters, in this life! The CHA Process is always available for anyone seeking support on their journey toward, healing, feeling, awakening, Self-Discovery, and Everlasting Liberation! True Self-Realization!

WILLINGNESS ABUNDANCE GRATITUDE

The Power of Sacred Processes

Like Meditation, Yoga, Nature Immersion, Self-Inquiry, and Centering Prayer

In today's fast-paced world, Sacred Processes offer profound benefits for overall well-being and Self-Discovery. Practices like meditation, yoga, centering prayer, nature immersion, and self-inquiry provide holistic healing for the mind, body, and spirit.

Meditation and centering prayer cultivate inner peace, reducing stress and enhancing mental clarity. Yoga, with its combination of physical postures and breath control, improves flexibility, strength, and balance, while nurturing emotional resilience and assisting with the healing qualities of somatic experiencing. Nature immersion reconnects us with the natural world, grounding our energy and promoting a sense of tranquility. Self- inquiry encourages deep reflection, helping to uncover belief systems no longer serving us while healing emotional wounds.

Together, these practices create a conscious approach to health, nurturing a balanced, harmonious life and fostering enduring well-being, healing, feeling, and awakening. (For basic guidance see pages 28-30.)

Visit www.DiscoverCHA.org for detailed information regarding Sacred Processes toward overall well-being.

Trust the Process

Almost everyone is unaware that underneath the mind's inner conflict, stress, fear, obsessions, identity struggles, and compulsions, there is everlasting wholeness; peaceful joyousness, an unshakable calm, pure serenity, unconditional love.
The Real YOU!

Awaiting your loving attention is this always complete, worthy, and whole sense of self already here now.

This is the essence of healing, feeling, and awakening.

True Recovery.
True Self-Discovery.
True Self-Realization.

GETTING STARTED IN

Empowering Non-Religious Spirituality toward Self-Discovery, Healing, and Awakening

Collective Healing Anonymous

GETTING STARTED in Collective Healing Anonymous is actually very simple: Read this basics book, start on the 30-day Life Principles Practice, Read the 12 steps everyday for 40 days, go to meetings, and the rest will fall into place as your willingness and readiness to heal, feel, and awaken continues unfolding.

Another way to get started is to contact the person who gave you this brochure or visit us online at: www.DiscoverCHA.org

Are you no longer interested in...

- being a slave to your mind, emotions, thoughts, beliefs, compulsions, obsessions?
- living in fear, guilt, inner conflict, or shame?
- feeling bad about yourself, not good enough?
- living the way you were taught, forced, programmed?
- suffering unworthiness and false sense of lack?

Are you open and interested in...

- discovering your authentic self & expression?
- feeling, healing, awakening, inner freedom, everlasting joy, peaceful coexistence, Self-Discovery?
- another way to be alive? Living in integrity?
- freedom from all obsessions, compulsions, addictions, and identity matters, IN THIS LIFE?

If you answer **YES to ANY** of the **following** questions then Collective Healing Anonymous **is** for you.

DO YOU OBSESS ABOUT...

- what others think of you? Your self-image?
- getting validation OR approval? Your credit score?
- conflicting beliefs or assumptions in the mind?
- feeling unwhole, incomplete, not enough?
- guilt, shame, fear, anger, OR unworthiness?
- people pleasing OR trying to make people happy at your own expense? Working?
- rejection, abandonment, being left behind?
- social media, checking your mobile device or watching television or videos? Gambling?
- how religion doesn't fit with your beliefs?
- fear of relapse? Acting out? Acting in?
- drinking alcohol, smoking pot, using illegal drugs OR taking legally prescribed medication?
- what your purpose in life is OR not fitting in?
- having sex, masturbating, or watching porn?
- getting affection, love, or appreciation?
- what you think others should be doing with their lives? Blaming others for your misery?
- politics OR religion OR certain people?
- making enough money or buying more stuff?
- judging others or yourself or mentally beating yourself up for not being good enough?
- talking, over-eating, thinking, over-analyzing?
- what happens when you die?
- being better than someone else? Interrupting?
- keeping secrets from people or yourself?
- how to love or allow yourself to be loved?
- the seeming ongoing chaos in the world?
- playing video games OR shooting guns?
- avoiding feeling your feelings and sensations?
- getting hurt or harming someone else?
- excitement and thrills OR what to do next?

The 12 Steps of CHA

1. We humbly acknowledge the impact of [the coping mechanism dependency] on our lives, understanding it is only temporary, and embrace the powers within us to reclaim autonomy of our minds.

2. We opened to the possibility that the power to restore conscious clarity resides within ourselves, and that we can utilize this Universal Loving Force and inner strength as Trust, Compassion, Gratitude, Diligent Focus, and Willingness, while utilizing relevant external guidance and support whenever we so choose.

3. Made a conscious decision to turn to and trust the deeper, silent wisdom and Universal Loving Intelligence within, choosing to rely on this inner guidance rather than being driven solely by our conditioning, mental will, thoughts, obsessions, and compulsions. By embracing this inner wisdom, our false identities gradually dissolve as awareness of our essential, already whole, inseparable being emerges.

4. By acknowledging our primal innocence, we made a compassionate and fearlessly honest inventory of self-judgments we have been carrying in the mind.

5. Admitted to our Universal Self, our personal self, and to another human being the exact nature of our believed self-judgments. (Hint: All three are one in the same.)

6. Were entirely ready to free ourselves from ALL self-criticism, self-judgment, self-blame, guilt, and unworthiness by allowing ourselves to feel whatever we have been avoiding.

7. Humbly sought inwardly through meditative self-inquiry to compassionately observe and understand the innocent nature of our beliefs, behaviors, feelings, and suffering.

8. Made a list of all persons we believe we have harmed and became willing to make amends to them all.

9. Made direct amends to such people wherever possible, except when to do so would injure them, others, or myself.

10. Continued to remain mindful and alert to unnecessary inner dialogue and judgmental thoughts, as well as externalized speech and behaviors; and when we believed we caused harm, promptly admitted it.

11. Sought through meditation, self-inquiry, and various other Sacred Processes to fully understand and become aware of the nature of suffering, experience, divine reality, and mySELF; thereby completely dissolving the illusion of separation and unwholeness.

12. Having become deeply healed and awakened through the power of awareness, we continue allowing life to effortlessly flow with ease, balance, and grace, while our lives effortlessly unfold beyond personal identity and both the illusion of control and separation.

To learn more about the Collective Healing Anonymous process and partcipate in gatherings, ask the person who gave you this brochure; or go to: www.DiscoverCHA.org

CHA
Collective Healing Anonymous

The CHA journey begins with the power of

ACKNOWLEDGEMENT

Through the power of acknowledging there is another way to be alive, we humbly open our hearts and minds to prioritizing a life of inner freedom, joyous peace and conscious clarity, rather than defaulting to avoidance, isolation, blame, and self-criticism; thereby reclaiming autonomy of the mind and body.

A Deeper Look into Collective Healing Anonymous (CHA)
A Compassionate Journey of Awakening Beyond Addiction & Dependency

In a world where suffering often feels like the norm, where people grapple with a myriad of addictions, dependency issues, and identity challenges, a profound evolution is underway. Collective Healing Anonymous (CHA) emerges as a groundbreaking non-religious process and community that transcends the limitations of traditional 12-step programs, offering a fresh perspective rooted in collective consciousness and deep introspection toward total liberation, healing, inner freedom, and full recovery from any and all addiction and dependency matters. We understand that you are not alone; that everyone is temporarily suffering from some type of addiction, coping mechanism, or dependency; and that this program is not for those who need it, but for those who freely choose it.

Collective Healing Anonymous (CHA) recognizes that addiction and dependency issues take many forms, and defines them more accurately as temporary coping mechanisms. Whether it's substance abuse, compulsive behaviors, emotional dependencies, or becoming dependent on untrue beliefs, CHA provides a sacred haven for compassionately acknowledging a variety of addictions, mental health challenges, dependencies, and personal identity crises. It understands that the human experience is complex, and the roots of dependency are diverse. By addressing the foundational causes of all forms of dependency, obsession, compulsion, and addiction, CHA ensures that no one is left behind on their journey toward healing and enlightenment, spiritual awakening. This inclusivity fosters a sense of unity, compassion, and understanding among participants, reinforcing the idea that we are all in this together, and no one is better or worse OR more worthy or unworthy than anyone else, regardless of the specific challenges we face or successes in our lives.

Embracing a Non-Religious Approach
CHA acknowledges that the path to healing and enlightenment should be open to all, irrespective of religious beliefs or any other affiliations; even if you consider yourself Atheist, Scientific, Agnostic, Christian, Muslim, Jewish, Hindu, or any other personal identity. It provides a universal framework that draws from the collective wisdom of humanity's diverse non-religious yet spiritual and non-spiritual traditions, even science; thereby emphasizing unity, compassion, and the inherent goodness and wholeness that we essentially are.

CHA as a Companion
Collective Healing Anonymous (CHA) is consciously designed to be a companion to any other 12-step or non 12-step program, counseling, or healing and awakening modalities. Unlike programs that demand exclusivity, CHA embraces inclusivity, recognizing that healing and growth can come from various sources. This flexibility allows individuals to integrate the CHA process with their existing practices, enhancing their overall journey. That is to say, CHA supports and complements other methods, providing an additional layer of depth and understanding. By not mandating exclusivity, CHA empowers individuals to create a personalized and holistic approach to their healing and awakening, fostering a more comprehensive and fulfilling path to self-discovery.

Unearthing the Root Causes
CHA delves to the core of obsessions, compulsions, addiction, and identity problems, recognizing that they are mere symptoms of deeper existential questions arising from the Primal Addiction of feeling fragmented or separate from the Universal Whole of Reality. It empowers us to explore the foundational causes of our suffering, which often manifest as temporary coping mechanisms, often arising from unresolved emotional distress, identity struggles, and societal conditioning. By shining a light on these underlying issues, CHA encourages a profound shift towards self-awareness and liberation; and full recovery, and awakening!

Embracing Willingness and Transformation

Willingness, as a cornerstone of CHA, invites us to embark on an inner journey, not only to overcome addictions, mental challenges, and dependency problems, but to discover the roots of all inner turmoil and the nature of reality and ourselves. It is the key to unlocking the doors of self-discovery, healing, and enlightenment, Self-Realization. Therefore, as well as attending support-group meetings, we willingly engage in deep introspection, embracing our inner wisdom, and reclaiming our power within.

A Sanctuary of Collective Wisdom

CHA creates a sacred space where we gather to share our stories, insights, and collective wisdom in a judgment-free environment. Here, the focus is not on labeling oneself as an "addict" but on recognizing the shared human experience of seeking answers to life's profound questions, as well as becoming aware of our unifying commonalities; thereby revitalizing our inherent and natural connection with one another. By actively participating and engaging with others who have walked similar paths, we gain a deeper understanding of ourselves, the nature of experience, and our struggles. The collective experiences of the group members contribute to a tapestry of support and empathy that is unparalleled. It reinforces the natural understanding or possibility that each individual has the potential for profound transformation and self-realization in this life, and that the necessary support and guidance is readily available.

Coming Out of Hiding

Participating in a group environment within Collective Healing Anonymous (CHA) holds profound significance as it symbolizes the act of "coming out of hiding" from the shackles of shame and guilt that bind us. Within the non-judgmental acceptance of the CHA community, we have the opportunity to openly share our experiences, vulnerabilities, and insights. This act of sharing is an essential step towards breaking free from the isolation that often accompanies identity challenges and addiction and dependency issues.

In the embrace of the CHA community, we find the strength to shed the layers of shame and secrecy that have held us captive. We emerge from hiding, allowing our authentic selves to shine forth, empowered, and harmonious, thereby reclaiming our inherent autonomy over our minds and bodies. This collective journey transcends dependency and addiction, fosters deep healing, and ultimately leads to the awakening of a more genuine and liberated, and complete sense of self.

From Surviving to Thriving

Collective Healing Anonymous invites all to move from merely surviving to thriving. It challenges the conventional narrative of dependency and addiction by reframing it as an invitation to awaken to our trueSELF, to understand the human condition, and to heal both individually and collectively. The program fosters evolving from living from a limiting perspective of self-preservation existing in basic survival mode, to maturing and flourishing unto higher, more authentic and fearless possibilities.

Changing the Narrative of Dependency and Addiction

In Collective Healing Anonymous (CHA), we recognize that dependency and addiction have long been stigmatized and misunderstood. We believe it is time to shift the conversation and reframe those ideas as what they truly are—temporary coping mechanism dependencies. And, dependencies that are NOT life-long afflictions nor identities, but opportunities to learn and grow; to feel, heal, and awaken. By acknowledging that all dependency issues, compulsions, obsessions, and addictions, whether they manifest as substance abuse or compulsive behaviors, which are rooted in the innocent human drive for temporary relief from inner pain and discomfort, we remove the judgment and 'shame blocks' often associated with those life restricting survival and coping strategies.

Furthermore, the CHA approach and understanding of healing and awakening recognizes that we innocently turn to coping mechanisms and survival strategies as a way to navigate our emotional and psychological challenges, and existential concerns. By shifting the traditional understanding, language, and perspective to one of mercy, deep introspection, and compassionate understanding, we more openly and willingly embrace the possibility of absolute healing and liberation from our obsessions, compulsions, dependency, and addiction matters, in this life. The CHA Process is always available for anyone seeking support on their journey toward, healing, feeling, awakening, and everlasting liberation.

Sacred Processes of Feeling, Healing, Awakening

CHA recognizes that true healing and awakening require a holistic approach that transcends the conventional paradigms of Self-Discovery and dependency and addiction recovery. For instance, meditation, yoga, nature immersion, and self-inquiry offer life-liberating techniques that uproot the causal factors of addiction and dependency problems. These practices also illuminate conscious clarity as our essential being awakens. Within the framework of these sacred processes, CHA encourages us to delve deep into our emotional landscapes, acknowledging and embracing our innermost feelings. This unearths the emotional wounds, unattended sorrow, and unresolved traumas that often underlie and sustain our temporary coping mechanisms manifesting as identity crises and addiction issues. By allowing ourselves to feel our spontaneous feelings, we are empowered to heal. CHA is not merely a means to overcome obsessions, compulsions, and identity challenges, but a path to self-realization and inner harmony.

Resource Open Mindedness

Resource open-mindedness is a fundamental principle of Collective Healing Anonymous (CHA). Unlike traditional programs, CHA encourages exploration beyond its own literature, fostering a holistic approach to healing and awakening. We understand that each individual's journey is unique, and what resonates for one person may differ for another. Therefore, we embrace a wide array of resources—spiritual teachers, scientific views, books, videos, and various forms of guidance. By remaining open-minded and open-hearted, we allow ourselves to utilize any and all tools that call to us. This inclusive approach ensures that we can tap into the most relevant and effective resources for our personal growth and spiritual development, nurturing a richer and more comprehensive path to healing and self-discovery.

All-Inclusive Membership

Unlike traditional 12-Step Programs like Alcoholics Anonymous and Al-Anon Family Groups, the qualification for membership in CHA does not have a limit. In AA the only criteria for membership is this, "A desire to stop drinking" and in Al-Anon, the only requirement is that you have been affected by someone else's drinking. Collective Healing Anonymous is fundamentally All-Inclusive and states the only requirement for involvement is that you are a human being; which means in that sense, everyone is already a member and can utilize the program regardless of whatever addiction, dependency, obsessions, compulsions, or identity challenges facing them. There will never be any dues, fees, or financial obligations of any kind to partipate in Collective Healing Anonymous.

You are already innocent, deserving, worthy, complete...always.

Of course you are already innocent. Of course acting out any addiction or coping mechanism is rooted in our original and primal innocence; because who could fault anyone for merely trying to feel better or innocently cope with the challenges, confusion, and wildness of the experience of life.

Humbly accept and embrace your natural innocence and wholeness. It never left.

Awareness, Awareness,

AWARENESS

Awareness is not a thought, feeling, emotion, or sensation; cannot be learned, earned, felt, acquired, believed, bought, or sold; yet effortlessly heals and liberates.

The Four Pillars of Collective Healing Anonymous

Active participation in the Collective Healing Anonymous process revolves around becoming willing to embrace four practical pillars: attending meetings, finding a journey advocate, wholeheartedly engaging in the steps, and diligently becoming willing to complete the healing exercises and Sacred Processes within the CHA books. Please understand that everything in CHA is a suggestion, not mandatory.

I. **Go to Meetings and Participate:** Attending CHA meetings marks the beginning of your conscious journey of healing, feeling, and awakening. Here, we start coming out of hiding, learning that by allowing ourselves to be vulnerable, we discover our deeper invulnerability. These sacred and supportive spaces help us trust another process rather than defaulting to our 'egoic-mind' that got us into trouble in the first place. We begin turning our attention toward the higher collective wisdom of the group and the deeper intelligence and stillness within our being. The false sense of disconnection starts to dissolve in the light of awareness as you connect with others who understand your struggles and aspirations. However, attending meetings is just the start; participation is key. Sharing your experiences, listening to others' stories, and engaging in discussions all contribute to the collective wisdom that fuels your progress.

II. **Find a Journey Advocate:** A journey advocate is someone in the program that you connect with on many levels, who can be your temporary guiding light through the darkness in the CHA journey, and provides a profound level of compassionate accountability that we may be unable to provide to ourselves just yet. They offer support, guidance, and a helping hand when you need it most. Finding a journey advocate who resonates with your experiences, understanding, and aspirations is pivotal. With their wisdom and encouragement, you'll have a compassionate ally to help you navigate the challenges and triumphs that come your way. Anyone can be a Journey Advocate for someone else, provided the same level of dedication and willingnes is present in both participants.

III. **Genuinely and Willingly Engaging in the Steps:** The heart of the CHA process lies in the steps. Wholeheartedly embracing the steps means facing them with an open heart and mind, willing to address and acknowledge whatever is necessary for feeling, healing, and awakening. This process naturally leads to the healing of your core wounds of unworthiness, unattended sorrow, innermost trauma, and unresolved grief, while simultaneously awakening to the joyously peaceful truth of you and the boundless potential of a brighter future. Your willingness to embrace each step is an act of self-empowerment, self-love, a conscious decision and affirmation that you're ready to transform your life with dedication, tenderness, self-honesty, and grace.

IV. **Complete the Exercises and Sacred Processes in the CHA Books:** Although everthing in CHA is a humble suggestion and not a rule, the exercises and Sacred Processes in the CHA books are carefully designed to facilitate your freedom from compulsions and identity challenges; and expedite your healing, transformation, and awakening. They provide you with a structured path to explore your inner-self, confront your inner conflicts, feel your feelings, and reclaim your joyous and already whole nature. Committing to these exercises and processes is a practical investment in your well-being, an act of self-compassion and self-love. CHA highly suggests making meditation a daily part of your life. (See Meditation Basics on page 28 in this CHA Basics Book.)

Meditation Basics

Meditation as a Sacred Process offers a powerful path to inner peace and self-awareness, and starting with simple techniques can make the journey accessible and rewarding. Beginners can cultivate mindfulness by focusing on the breath, tuning into the constant presence of inner peace, or observing physical sensations with compassionate interest; thereby reducing stress and anxiety while enhancing our powers of observation and overall well-being. This guide provides easy-to-follow steps to help you embark on your meditation journey, fostering a deeper connection with your inner being while promoting relaxation, emotional balance, and most importantly, awareness, awareness, awareness.

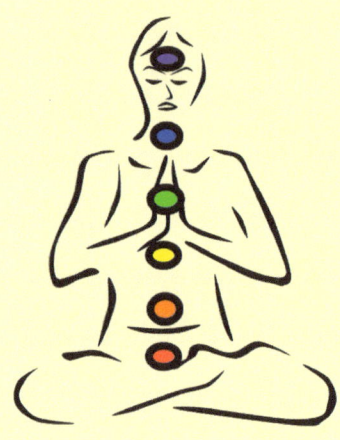

Getting Started in Meditation or Exploring Meditative Options

For those of us new to meditation, starting with simple techniques can be highly effective. One suggested method is to close your eyes and rest your attention on the sensation of your breath at the tip of your nose. Notice the impermanent nature of the cool air entering in, and warm air flowing out. As you do this, observe the fleeting activity of your mind - the impermanent nature of thought. If you notice your attention wandering, gently bring your focus back to the breath sensation at the end of your nose. This practice helps cultivate mindfulness and concentration.

Another option is to close your eyes and become aware of the peace beneath all thoughts and experiencing, a constant loving presence within that is always here. Simply notice the permanent unchanging peace amid the mental and emotional activty, or feelings and sensations that are constantly changing, shifting.

Alternatively, you can focus on physical sensations in your body. Close your eyes and place your attention on areas that feel tense, contracted, or tight, such as a knot in the stomach or tightness in the chest or shoulders. Observe these sensations with compassionate interest, noticing how they move and change. This practice promotes body awareness and emotional release.

These simple meditation techniques can help you develop a deeper connection with your natural, whole sense of self, while fostering relaxation and emotional well-being; as well as allowing helpful and healing insights to arise.

Overcoming Resistance to Meditation

Resistance to meditation is a common challenge, often fueled by the ego-mind's tendency to distract us from self-awareness. The ego-mind can weave intricate stories, convincing us that we are too busy, restless, or unprepared for meditation. These narratives serve as barriers, preventing us from realizing how much our thoughts control us.

To overcome this resistance, it is essential to recognize these mental patterns without judgment. Acknowledge the mind's stories and gently guide your focus back to your meditation practice. Understand that discomfort and distraction are natural parts of the process, signaling areas where loving, kind, and curious attention is being sought.

Commit to short, consistent meditation sessions, gradually increasing the duration as you build your practice. Celebrate small victories and maintain a compassionate attitude toward yourself. By persistently returning attention to your breath, inner peace, or bodily sensations, you gradually diminish the ego-mind's control, opening up deeper self-awareness and tranquility; thereby consciously reclaiming autonomy of the body-mind.

Yoga Basics

Yoga is often misconceived as merely a form of exercise focused on stretching and improving flexibility. However, its origins are deeply rooted in the practice of Kriya Yoga, which emphasizes spiritual growth and self-realization. Kriya Yoga involves a variety of techniques designed to accelerate spiritual evolution through the breath. This ancient practice aims to harmonize the body, mind, and spirit, extending far beyond the physical benefits typically associated with modern yoga routines.

Hatha Yoga, a prominent branch of yoga, primarily concentrates on enhancing the physical body. This practice includes a variety of asanas (postures) and pranayama (breathing exercises) aimed at increasing strength, flexibility, and balance. Unlike Kriya Yoga, which focuses on spiritual growth, Hatha Yoga's primary goal is to prepare the body for deeper meditation and spiritual realizations by maintaining health and vitality. Through compassionate physical practice, Hatha Yoga seeks to create a strong and purified body, which serves as a foundation for mental clarity and spiritual progress.

Fundamentally, yoga means union—an inseparable reality that exists here now. Any practice, technique, or act of surrender that reveals one's inherent wholeness, completeness, and unity with and as the entire cosmos is yoga itself. This profound realization transcends the physical and spiritual distinctions of various yoga practices, emphasizing that true yoga is the recognition of our ultimate nature, as the universe itSELF.

Suggested Yoga Practices

Connecting With the Breath throughout the day, as often as one remembers, is a simple yet profound form of yoga. This practice helps anchor the mind in the present moment, fostering a sense of calm and awareness. By mindfully observing each breath, one can cultivate a deeper connection with the self and the surrounding world, embodying the essence of yoga in daily life.

Embracing the Mantra "I am not the body; I am not even the mind" is a powerful yogic practice. This affirmation helps transcend physical and mental limitations, guiding one towards the realization of their true, eternal nature. By internalizing this wisdom, one can experience a profound sense of freedom and unity with and as universal consciousness.

Popular Hatha Yoga Postures

Child's Pose   Warrior Pose   Sitting Pose

Self-Inquiry Basics

Self-inquiry is a profound practice centered on asking introspective questions to uncover one's true nature while healing emotional patterns and dissolving belief habits no longer serving us. This process typically involves inwardly questioning the beliefs and assumptions we hold about ourselves, such as "Who am I?" or "Is this belief truly accurate and reliable?" By examining these beliefs, we begin to discern whether they are genuine or merely constructs of the ego-mind. Through this deep and reflective questioning, self-inquiry helps to dismantle illusions and misperceptions, allowing us to discover a more authentic sense of self, purpose, and meaning.

Suggested Self Inquiry Questions
Guidance toward Allowing Life to be Exactly as it is

Beyond Rationalizing Pain and Suffering: If it were a choice, would I rather be happy, joyous, and peaceful NOW for NO reason, or later for a reason? What am I presently choosing? How so? What is my direct experience right now?

Direct Reality beyond Limitations of Obsessing: In my direct experience, is it even possible to suffer DIRECT reality, OR am I suffering my interpretation, unreal expectations, and avoidance of reality? HOW so?

Befriending Experience: What is my ongoing experience of allowing and trusting the unreliable process of THINKING to be priority in my life over directly FEELING life? How am I resisting spontaneous Joy & Appreciation?

Empowerment and Trust: Am I open to discovering that my serenity is 100% my responsibility? If that were true, would I be more or less trusting of a Higher Power/Life/God/Myself? How so?

Freedom from Procrastination: Am I waiting for someone else, a situation, or a condition to be met in order to allow happiness and contentment to illuminate itself from within? Has waiting for a reason to be 'mySELF' right now ever provided the peace I am seeking?

Beyond the Illusion of Fear: Have I 'survived' my greatest fears and feelings I have been avoiding for most of my life? So, then, if you are still here, what is there to be afraid of? If I befriend fear, where can it be found?

Befriending Life Experience: If I befriend my painful or joyous feelings and place my attention on sensations, what happens? What is the reality? What happens if I befriend my direct experience of Life?

On Self-Sabotaging: Does the illusion of fear arise when I become willing to be quiet, meditate, or walk alone in nature? How am I believing the self-defeating stories in the mind which sabotage trusting stillness, inner peace, happiness here, now?

The Unreliability of Trusting the Energy of Judging: When I trust the thoughts, voices, or beliefs of self-judgment, self-punishment, or blame, what is my experience? How does it feel? Is it worth it?

Letting Go and Inclusion: What am I willing to let go in order to discover RELIABLE inner peace WITHIN? Here now? What am I willing to include? Right here, right now?

CHA is about embracing Your Superpowers of...

...compassion, discernment, attention, acknowledgment, humility, self-honesty, willingness, humor, acceptance, forgiveness, gratitude, trust, awareness, presence, courage, openness, clarity, love, patience, integrity, surrender, grace, conscious choice.

Your Toolbox of Resources

Suggested Books by Category

Self-Realization and Enlightenment

A New Earth: Awakening Your Life's Purpose by Eckhart Tolle

Inner Engineering: A Yogi's Guide to Joy by Sadhguru

Letting Go: The Pathway of Surrender by David Hawkins

Being Aware of Being Aware by Rupert Spira

Toward a Psychology of Awakening: Buddhism, Psychotherapy, and the Path of Personal and Spiritual Transformation by John Welwood

Falling into Grace: Insights on the End of Suffering by Adyashanti

Awareness: The Perils and Opportunities of Reality by Anthony De Mello

Loving What Is, Revised Edition: Four Questions That Can Change Your Life; The Revolutionary Process Called "The Work" by Byron Katie

The Diamond in Your Pocket: Discovering Your True Radiance by Gangaji

Love, Freedom, Aloneness: The Koan of Relationships by OSHO

Before I Am, Second Edition: The Direct Recognition of Truth by Mooji

I Am That by Nisargadatta Maharaj

The Book of Awakening by Mark Nepo

The Four Agreements: A Practical Guide to Personal Freedom by Don Miguel Ruiz

Healing Shame, Self-Hate, and Unworthiness

There is Nothing Wrong with You by Cheri Huber

Facing Shame - Families in Recovery by Merle Fossum & Marilyn Mason

Homecoming: Reclaiming and Championing Your Inner Child by John Bradshaw

The Gifts of Imperfection: 10th Anniversary Edition by Brene Brown

Evolve Your Brain: The Science of Changing Your Mind by Dr. Joe Dispenza

Recovering from Religion

Conversations with God: An Uncommon Dialogue Books 1, 2, and 3 by Neale Donald Walsh

Grief Recovery

The Grief Recovery Handbook: 20th Anniversary Edition by John W. James & Russell Friedman

Trauma Healing & Somatic Experiencing

Attuned: Practicing Interdependence to Heal Our Trauma and Our World by Thomas Hubl

The Body Keeps the Score: Brain, Mind, and Body in the Healing of Trauma by Bessel Van Der Kolk

Healing Collective Trauma: A Process for Integrating our Intergenerational & Cultural Wounds by Thomas Hubl

In an Unspoken Voice: How the Body Releases Trauma and Restores Goodness by Peter A. Levine

The Myth of Normal: Trauma, Illness & Healing in a Toxic Culture by Gabor Mate

Complex PTSD: From Surviving to Thriving: A Guide and Map for Recovering from Childhood Trauma by Pete Walker

Psychology, Chronic Pain & Emotional Healing

The Mindbody Prescription: Healing the Body, Healing the Pain by John E. Sarno, M.D.

Heal Your Body: The Mental Causes for Physical Illness and the Metaphysical Way to Overcome Them by Louise Hay

12-Step Recovery (without the god concept)

Trauma and the 12 Steps, Revised and Expanded: An Inclusive Guide to Enhancing Recovery by Jamie Marisch

Buddhism & the Twelve Steps Daily Reflections: Thoughts on Dharma and Recovery by Kevin Griffen

Beyond Belief: Agnostic Musings for 12-Step Life: finally, a daily reflection book for nonbelievers, freethinkers and everyone by Joe. C

12-Step Recovery (with the god concept)

Breathing Under Water: Spirituality and the 12 Steps by Richard Rohr

Soul Recovery - 12 Keys to Healing Dependence: The 12 Steps for the Rest of Us—A Path to Wholeness, Serenity and Success by Ester Nicholson

The AA Big Book Fifth Edition by Alcoholics Anonymous

Adult Children: Alcoholic / Dysfunctional Families by Adult Children of Alcoholics

Courage to Change Daily Reader by Al-Anon Family Groups

Online Resources & Directories

Access and links to the most updated resources and directories can be found at: www.discoverCHA.org.

Self-Realization and Enlightenment

This *Sacred Guidance Directory* provided by Peace President United links you directly to a comprehensive list of todays most awakened non-religious spiritual teachers and enlightened masters. As many spiritual teachings become lost in religious dogma, this directory links you to a comprehensive list of teachers specifically relating to healing, feeling, awakening, Self-Discovery, and Self-Realization - Enlightenment; beyond the confines of traditional institutions and doctrine. Visit: www.peacepresidentunited.org/gap/sacred-guidance-directory

Sacred Prcessess like Meditation & Yoga

Showcasing some of today's most trustworthy spiritual masters, this *Online Sacred Processes Guide* offers profound insights and teachings about a variety of healing and awakening techniques and methods, including: Meditation, Yoga, Introspective Self-Inquiry, Surrender, Nature Immersion, Receptive Silence, Embracing Joy, and Centering Prayer. Visit: www.peacepresidentunited.org/gap/sacred-processes-of-awakening

Self-Inquiry Method by Byron Katie

Byron Katie is an American spiritual teacher, best known for her method of self-inquiry known as "The Work." In 1986, she experienced a life-transforming realization from which her method arose. It is a simple yet powerful process of questioning and understanding the thoughts that cause personal suffering. Visit: www.thework.com

Trauma Awareness and Healing

Discover a curated collection of videos, articles, links, and expert insights designed to guide you through the complexities of trauma recovery; including both PTSD and Complex-PTSD guidance. Whether you're seeking to understand personal trauma or the intergenerational effects of past events, our platform provides access to leading psychologists, therapists, and spiritual guides who offer cutting-edge techniques and compassionate support. Visit: www.peacepresidentunited.org/gap/befriending-and-healing-trauma

Peace President's Global Awareness Project

In a world clouded by misinformation, divisive narratives, and conflicting information from media, government, religion, and education, it is challenging to find reliable and trustworthy guidance toward collective unity, inner clarity, healing, addiction recovery, and peace. Amid this confusion, Peace President's Global Awareness Project aims to mend individual and collective trust issues, bridge social divides, and heal individual, generational, and collective wounds by offering consciously vetted and trustworthy information, guidance, and resources toward Collective Awareness, Inner Transformation, and Peaceful Coexistence. Visit: www.peacepresidentunited.org/gap

Guiding Principals of CHA

CHA is a Collective Movement: Collective Healing Anonymous is a Collective Movement toward feeling, healing, and awakening; neither a legal entity nor organization; and managed 100% by active participants on a volunteer basis; although the creation of temporary committees, project groups, and service boards may be utilized when relevant. Let us also understand and appreciate that CHA is not a belief system, philosophy, and not a religious teaching; does not ascribe to any single doctrine, guru, or spiritual master. It is, however, a supportive non-religious spiritual process and community focused on individual and collective healing through inner transformation and Self-Discovery using a variety of resources.

CHA is Fully Self-Supporting: Collective Healing Anonymous (CHA) is fully self-supporting through voluntary contributions as to not succomb to self-defeating influences of the external world. There will never be any dues, fees, or finanacial obligations of any kind in order to participate. CHA is a spiritual movement, not an organization, and not affiliated with any business, religion, sect, nation, government, or organization. And, to maintain our primary spiritual aim, all financial contributions are used exclusively for literature, meeting handouts, rent for meeting space when applicable, and other practical and essential expenses.

Attraction Rather than Promotion: The growth of Collective Healing Anonymous (CHA) is rooted in the principle of attraction rather than active promotion, marketing, and advertising. By embodying the values and transformative experiences of CHA, we naturally draw others who seek similar healing and awakening. Our focus is on living authentically, openly, and lovingly, allowing our personal and spiritual growth and positive changes to inspire and attract others to our collective journey. This ensures that those who come to CHA do so out of genuine interest and attraction. The *CHA Basics Book* is designed to be shared with anyone interested in learning more about Collective Healing Anonymous and may be used as a psuedo marketing piece or gift.

How to Conduct a Basic CHA Gathering?
Collective Healing Anonymous Support Group Gathering Guidelines

The information below are guidelines for the leader of the CHA gathering to successfully and eloquently conduct a meeting. To preserve the intimate nature of our gatherings, the setting is always to be non-public. Venues may include a personal residence, private office space, recovery building, meditation center, yoga studio, or in nature. In special circumstances, a room at a church, hospital, or private area in a library or community center may be used. Meetings last 1 hour, and it is important to begin and end on time.

Suggested Meeting Format

- **Arrival:** Basic meet and greet as people arrive and talk amongst themselves before the gathering.

- **Getting Started:** Leader requests attention for everyone to gather and sit down. (Note this: often participants find great benefits after the meeting by talking amongst themselves. So if applicable and the meeting space is available, feel free to let them know they do not have to hurry out after the gathering.)

- **Announcements:** Ask this: Before we get started are there any CHA group related announcements? [Note: CHA's aim is for everyone to receive a copy of the CHA Basics Book at their very first meeting or prior to attending, so ask if everyone has received a copy or purchased one online? ($15 min. donation.)]

- **CHA is Fully Self Supporting:** Read this: It is important to understand that CHA is a spiritual movement, not an organization, and not affiliated with any business, religion, sect, nation, government, or organization. We are fully self-supporting through voluntary contributions, although there will never be any dues, fees, or finanacial obligations of any kind in order to participate. To maintain our primary spiritual aim, all financial contributions are used exclusively for creating and publishing literature, rent for meeting space when applicable, and any other practical and essential expenses that support us. (Set out or pass the contribution basket.)

- **Official Opening:** Read or ask someone to read the suggested CHA meeting introduction. Encourage attendees to read along in their CHA Literature; for instance, the *CHA Basics Book*.

- **Meditation Period:** 7 minute silent meditation.

- **Read this Reminder of Sharing:** As we move into our discussion time, let us honor some specific guidelines so everyone feels comfortable sharing. (1) No one is to comment or offer advice except when the person sharing asks for feedback or advice. (2) Although verbal participation is highly encouraged, know that your participation is completely optional; which means you may choose to pass at any time. (3) Anything said during our meetings is held in utmost confidence and is to stay within our trusted circle. And (4) The group leader is responsible for helping participants observe and honor our guidelines and follow the meeting format.

- **Introductions:** Read this: Let's go around the circle and introduce ourselves by first name only; and to honor our discussion time, briefly state in one or two sentences why you feel you are here today.

- **Specific Intentions:** Read this: Let's go around the circle again and in 60 seconds or less, share if there are any specific obsessions, compulsions, addictions, or identity challenges you are seeking to heal and liberate. (Note: Sometimes people may talk longer which is fine, but be mindful to maintain the format.)

- **Discussion Period:** Although a specific topic is not mandatory, one can be established by the leader or by asking the attendees this: Does anyone have a topic relating to healing, feeling, and awakening you would like to discuss? For instance, being authentic, letting go of negative self-talk, the power of gratitude, overcoming feelings of unworthiness and shame, challenges with allowing ourselves to embrace, feel, and express joy and gratitude, committing to a daily spiritual practice like meditation or yoga. (See Suggested Discussion Options for Meetings in the *CHA Basics Book* on page 36, if necessary).

- **Suggested Closing & Gratitude Circle:** Read the suggested CHA closing.

Suggested Meeting Introduction

Welcome to our 1 hour Collective Healing Anonymous gathering toward feeling, healing, and awakening. Before we begin, let us take a moment and acknowledge the life-liberating Powers of Gratitude and Humility, understanding that our presence here is a loving gesture to open our hearts and minds to discovering the ultimate truth of our being. And of course, by attending these meetings, we are calling attention to our sincere interest in freedom from all obsession, compulsion, and addiction matters.

CHA differs from traditional 12-step processes by taking a more liberating, holistic, and universal approach to healing, feeling, and awakening. It is a non-religious, yet highly spiritual 12-step process focused on inner transformation and self discovery, which we tenderly unveil as we compassionately acknowledge and heal underlying addictions and dependencies no longer serving us. Foundationally, we understand that our self-defeating and self-sabotaging obsessions, compulsions, and identity challenges take many forms, and more accurately define them as [temporary coping mechanisms]—which can absolutely be healed and liberated—in this Life! That is to say, the CHA healing and awakening process is not about creating identities that resign to lifelong struggles, but true liberation from all suffering in the here and now!

For those of us who are new to the CHA community, support group, and 12-step process, we recognize that all coping mechanisms and habits are a type of avoidance and share commonalities; and not limited to the consumption of substances or engagement in compulsive behaviors. Whether one's [temporary coping mechanisms] no longer serving them are substance abuse, compulsive behaviors, emotional dependencies, self judgment, complaining, negativity, attachment to relationships, reliance on untrue beliefs, or a combination of them, CHA provides a sacred haven for anyone struggling with any variety of addictions, painful habits, or personal identity crises.

We are like-minded and compassionate beings sincerely interested in connection, thinking for ourselves, and genuine self exploration, healing, and awakening. Through compassionate self-honesty and by supporting and encouraging one another in a judgment-free environment, our mutual caring will naturally dissolve our egoic defenses. And although our time together nurtures a deeper spiritual connection with others, we understand what we are ultimately seeking is already within. By attending meetings, following the steps, and by tapping into the collective wisdom and experience of the group, we embark on a journey of self-discovery, healing, and transformation.

Before moving on with the discussion period, we will now have a short 7 minute silent meditation. And for those who are new to meditation or seeking guidance, there is a meditation section in the *CHA Basics Book*; or feel free to speak with someone after the meeting.

Collective Healing Anonymous Dedication

CHA is a loving invitation and compassionate opportunity to be deeply honest with ourselves through a revolutionary non-religious 12-step process toward healing, feeling, and awakening. As we begin realizing our primal innocence and truth of ourselves through this journey of self-love, forgiveness, and acceptance, we rediscover our natural wholeness and worthiness that never left. By sincerely acknowledging and healing whatever obsessions, compulsions, addictions, and identity challenges holding us back from living a life of everlasting inner freedom and joyful peacefulness, we reclaim autonomy of our body and mind. As willing and grateful participants of CHA, we dedicate ourselves to genuine inner transformation, peaceful coexistence, and Self-Realization - Enlightenment.

Suggested Meeting Closing

As we conclude our gathering of Collective Healing Anonymous, let us take a moment to feel our sincere thanks for everyone here today. Your presence is not only a testament to your commitment to healing, feeling, and awakening, but a dedication and conscious decision to be free from any and all temporary coping mechanisms and identity challenges.

CHA is a supportive, non-religious spiritual process and community focused on individual and collective healing through inner transformation and Self-Discovery. Let us also understand and appreciate that CHA is not a belief system, philosophy, and not a religious teaching; does not ascribe to any single doctrine, guru, or spiritual master. That is to say, we remain forever open-minded to any resources, guidance, and wisdom that may work for us.

A special message to those of you who are new, and perhaps, were unsure about attending for the first time, or reluctant to come back. There are many of us who also felt the same way. Yet, as we continued to trust the process, we developed new friends and found the loving support, healing, and connection we have been seeking for most of our lives. We encourage you to read the *CHA Basics*, speak with someone after the meeting, and perhaps exchange phone numbers.

For all who care to join, let's stand together in a circle and hold hands in silence, while allowing gratitude and appreciative joy to fill our hearts and minds.

Optional Discussion Topics for Meetings

- Understanding that addictive habits, obsessions, and compulsions are merely innocent coping mechanisms, which are temporary, that seemingly mask or veil the underlying truth of ourselves, get in the way of living authentically, and restrict one's true expression from effortlessly unfolding.
- Each person shares about one or more of their coping mechanisms, how it is affecting their life, and their willingness and or resistance to heal and awaken from those dependencies and addictions.
- Current spiritual progress, new insights, realizations, or profound understandings.
- Go through the CHA Basics Book or other CHA literature, read a section and discuss it. For instance, the foundational themes of CHA.
- Not taking life too seriously. Giving ourselves permission to lighten up.
- Identity challenges and attachment to personal self-images and self-concepts no longer serving us.
- Compassionately acknowledging self-hate, self-judgment, and how we mentally beat ourselves up.
- We often become lost in what isn't working so let's discuss and appreciate everything that is going right in our lives; from what we consider the small things to everything else. It's truly amazing.
- Choose a step, read it, and open up the discussion.
- Choose and read a section, paragraph, or page in one of the suggested books in the Tool Box; then open up the discussion. Or, choose one or two off the Life-Principles Practices and discuss them.
- The importance of The Four Pillars of Collective Healing Anonymous: 1) Go to meetings and participate, (2) Find a Journey Advocate, (3) Genuinely and willingly engage in the Steps, and (4) Complete the exercises, practices, and Sacred Processes from the CHA Workbook; i.e. Meditation, Self-Inquiry, Nature Immersion, Yoga, etc.
- Choosing and committing to a daily spiritual practice such as meditation.
- (1) Bring to mind a person, belief, feeling, emotion, or situation that you are secretly holding resentment and judgment towards. (2) How does it feel to hold onto this resistance? (3) Ask yourself, are you ready to be free from this burden? (4) What is your process for being free from this? (5) Asking for help as compassionate accountability from someone to assist or encourage the process.
- What is my daily spiritual practice? The importance of including meditation in my life? Asking for support and accountability to maintain a consistent daily spiritual practice.

How to Start a CHA Gathering - Support Group?
Basic Instructions for Inviting Potential Participants

Starting a Collective Healing Anonymous (CHA) gathering can be a deeply rewarding experience, nurturing a sense of community and mutual support. To help guide you through the process, we have created a to-do list outlining the essential steps. This list will provide practical advice on how to initiate and sustain a CHA gathering, from identifying potential participants to creating a supportive environment. By following these steps, you will be well on your way to establishing a Sacred Space where individuals can come together to heal, grow, and support one another on their journey of self-discovery, and individual and collective awakening.

The To-Do List

1. **Thoroughly Read the CHA Basics Book:** Read and become deeply familiar with the entire CHA Basics Book; especially the *Four Pillars* and all of the *Tool Box Resources*, and specifically the *Guiding Principles* and *How to Conduct a Meeting* sections.

2. **Make a List of Potential Attendees:** Identify friends, family, coworkers, colleagues, and community members who might be interested in CHA, who have expressed interest in self-discovery, healing, inner transformation, enlightenment, or freedom from addiction, obsessions, compulsions, or identity challenges.

3. **Set a Date, Time, and Location:** Establish a recurring day of the week, time, and location. Evening times like Thursday or Friday at 7 pm are often popular. You may ask those interested about their best days and times. And feel free to change the day and or time after the meetings begin, if feedback suggests a better option.
   - Choose a private, comfortable and accessible location. To preserve the intimate nature of our meetings, the venue is to be a personal residence, private office space, recovery center, or a meditation or yoga center, or in nature. In special circumstances, a room at a church, library, or community center may be used. Make sure there would be adequate seating for at least 10 people.

4. **1st MSG - Create an Engaging Invitation:** DO NOT SEND GROUP MESSAGES, EVER. All messages are to be one person to one person. Send first MSG via text, email, by phone or in person, or word of mouth. (Sample messages can be found at www.DiscoverCHA.org/starting-a-meeting.)
   - Keep a list of who you have contacted and make sure to keep track of who is interested so you do not accidentally re-contact someone not interested. Note that it is okay for people not to confirm but show up; even show up late; which is often the case.
   - You may also purchase some CHA Basics Books and give one to anyone from your list as it can act as a basic, yet thorough, description of CHA, and brochure or marketing piece. (Request a $10 minimum contribution for those who can afford it, or give them away if there is enough money from prior donations.)

5. **2nd MSG - Reminder Follow Up After Initial Contact:** Reach out to people who expressed interest or didn't respond to the 1st MSG, letting them know the day, time, date, and location of the meeting. (Sample messages can be found at www.DiscoverCHA.org/starting-a-meeting.)

6. **Final MSG - Reminder:** On the day of the meeting, send a final reminder to anyone who has confirmed or expressed interest OR hasn't responded to prior messages. Be sure to include any location details to finding the meeting room or space. (Sample messages can be found at www.DiscoverCHA.org/starting-a-meeting.)
   - Note: It is not that uncommon to have only 2 or 3 people when beginning. Simply stay the course and more people will slowly trickle in. This is NOT a sprint, but a journey with no specific timeline.

7. **Prepare the Meeting Space:** Put out signs (handwritten is fine) if necessary. Arrange seating and materials to create a welcoming environment. Often, you will find that some people like to sit on the floor; especially for meditation.

8. **Conduct the meeting:** using the CHA Guidelines and format for *How to Conduct a Basic CHA Gathering*.

9. **Gather Feedback:** After the first meeting, ask attendees for their feedback and suggestions. Use this feedback to improve future gatherings.

30-Day Life-Principles Practice

Starting with #1, practice ONLY one principle for 30 days, as often as you can everyday, before moving to the next. Repeat for each principle exercise.

1 **Honoring gratitude and joyous appreciation.** This exercise involves honoring gratitude and joyous appreciation by taking time each day to acknowledge and celebrate the positive aspects of our lives, allowing us to be thankful for the beauty in both small and significant moments.

2 **Compassionate Self-Talk.** Throughout the day, pay attention to your inner dialogue. Notice any self-judging thoughts or self-critical voices that arise. When you identify one, pause and take a deep breath. Notice how it feels; and perhaps, replace the critical thought with a kind and compassionate statement.

3 **Opening to trust.** Opening to trust involves recognizing and appreciating the many aspects of life we already rely on without realizing it, such as the steady beat of our hearts, the rising of the sun each morning, that we will wake up in the morning, the support of loved ones, and so forth.

4 **Acknowledging our primal innocence by asking for help.** This principle is about recognizing that seeking support is a natural and courageous act, free from shame or guilt. By embracing our vulnerability and reaching out, we honor our fundamental innocence and humanity, fostering deeper connections and enabling growth and healing.

5 **Telling the Truth.** Telling the truth involves sharing our authentic selves with honesty and integrity, embracing both our strengths and vulnerabilities. It means speaking from the heart, free from the filters of fear or shame, and creating a foundation of trust and transparency in our relationships.

6 **Humbly giving ourselves permission to feel.** This exercise involves embracing our emotions and feelings without judgment or suppression, acknowledging them as valid and essential parts of our human experience. It allows us to connect with our inner experience more deeply and compassionately.

7 **Observing and questioning beliefs, assumptions, and thoughts.** Observing and questioning beliefs and thoughts entails adopting a stance of curious detachment towards our mental processes. By examining our thoughts, assumptions, and beliefs without immediate dislike or rejection, we discover new insights while uncovering underlying judgments and biases; as well as hidden joy and peace - serenity.

8 **Compassionately taking responsibility for our actions.** This exercise is about acknowledging with kindness and understanding that our actions affect ourselves and others. It encourages us to be conscious of our behavior without self-judgment, fear, hate, and contempt.

9 **Spontaneous forgiveness of ourselves and others.** This is a practice of releasing the burden of resentment and blame without the need for prolonged contemplation or analysis. It involves a natural and immediate letting go of grievances, allowing for peace and healing to enter our hearts.

10 **Loving, humble, and humorous accountability for ourselves.** This exercise involves not taking ourselves so seriously as we make our way through life. This practical principle also helps us recognize our role in creating our experiences, and learning from our words and actions without harsh self-judgment; fostering a sense of personal responsibility rooted in self-love and understanding.

11 **Willingly engaging in intentional quietude. Allowing, Observing, Breathing.** This practice is about creating space for stillness and introspection in our lives. It's about allowing ourselves to be present in the moment, observing our thoughts and feelings without judgment, and placing our kind attention on our breathing and sensations in the body. This principle encourages us to embrace the powers of silence, observation, and discernment as a means of deepening our self-awareness and connecting with our inner wisdom.

12 **Noticing the okayness of everything.** Noticing the okayness of everything is a practice of recognizing and accepting the inherent perfection of each moment as it is, without needing to change or control anything. It's about acknowledging that everything, including our thoughts, feelings, emotions, and external circumstances - all experience, is fundamentally okay just as it is.

To learn more about the Collective Healing Anonymous process and participate in gatherings, ask the person who gave you this brochure; or go to: www.DiscoverCHA.org

CHA
Collective Healing Anonymous

Prior to resistance is the freedom of
ALLOWING

Appreciating Now
Noticing - Feeling - Allowing

> **You are this moment.**
>
> ---
>
> *By acknowledging and valuing what is working in our lives, no matter how small or seemingly insignificant, instantly removes the illusion of fear, separation and disconnection from life.*

In our fast-paced, goal-oriented world, it's easy to become consumed with what we assume isn't working, what we think we lack, or how we falsely believe we fall short in one way or another. We often find ourselves lost in a cycle of judgment and criticism, unable to appreciate what is unfolding right here, now—as well as the positive aspects of our lives—the timeless present moment. This mindset of innocently ignoring unconditional loving reality not only masks our ever-present peace, but also blinds us from many qualities that *are* working in our lives, alongside the small acts of self-love we perform daily. Honestly and earnestly inquiring into the nature of mind proves that trying to find out who we are by allowing ourselves to believe and identify with its protective, divisive, and defensive instincts, does not, will not, and cannot provide the everlasting sense of wholeness we are seeking. Our lives are the living proof.

The Trap of Constant Inner and Outer Criticism

Our minds are wired to focus on problems and potential threats. While identifying with self-preservation tactics of mind was useful for survival in the past, it leads to a never-ending loop of dissatisfaction in modern life. When we constantly judge and criticize ourselves and our circumstances, we overlook the beauty of pure presence; and the healing, feeling, and awakening progress we have made. This incessant mental chatter creates a type of psychological fog to experiencing true joy and contentment without resistance.

Embracing Pure Presence

To break free from any cycles of avoidance, self-hate, or blame, by allowing ourselves to call attention to the present moment and cultivate and feel appreciation for what is right before our very eyes, can be helpful. This means acknowledging and valuing what is genuninely working in our lives, no matter how small or seemingly insignificant. By shifting our focus from what's missing to what we have, we open ourselves up to a more fulfilling and peaceful existence.

Exercises to Cultivate Presence, Appreciation, and Self-Awareness

Here are three journaling exercises designed to help you appreciate the present moment and recognize the ways in which you are already engaging in self-love, willingness, and healing. You will need a notebook and a pen.

Exercise 1: Willingness to Heal and Transform

Take a moment to acknowledge your willingness to heal and transform. The very act of reading this book, engaging with transformational material, or participating in Sacred Processes (like yoga or meditation) is a testament to your commitment to healing and awakening. Reflect on the following prompts:

- How have you shown a willingness to heal and transform in your life?
- What steps have you taken, no matter how small, toward personal and spiritual growth?
- How does engaging with this material reflect your commitment to healing, feeling, and awakening?
- Journal Prompt: "By reading this book and partaking in these exercises, I am demonstrating my willingness to heal and transform. Here are some other ways I have shown this willingness in my life..."

Exercise 2: Recognizing Acts of Self-Love

We often overlook the small acts of self-love that we perform daily. These actions, whether they are as simple as feeding our bodies, putting on clothes, or greeting someone with a smile, are essential to our well-being. Reflect on the following prompts:

- What daily routines do you engage in that contribute to your well-being?
- How do these routines reflect self-love?
- Can you identify any innocent coping mechanisms that you use to feel better? How might these also be seen as acts of self-love?
- Journal Prompt: "Here are some daily actions I take that reflect self-love, even if they are small or seem insignificant..."

Exercise 3: Understanding the Need for Validation

One of our earliest and deepest coping mechanisms is the need for validation. This need often drives us to seek approval from others and can lead to feelings of inadequacy when not met. Reflect on the following prompts:

- What is validation to you, and how does it manifest in your life?
- How often do you seek validation from others? From yourself?
- What do you feel when you receive validation? Does this feeling last? Is it ever completely fulfilling?
- How might you begin to provide validation for yourself instead of relying on external sources?
- Journal Prompt: "Validation shows up in my life as... I seek validation when... The feeling of validation lasts for... To provide validation for myself, I could..."

Appreciating Pure Presence, this-here-now, appears to require a shift in focus from what's missing to what is. By acknowledging our willingness to heal and recognizing our daily acts of self-love we become aware of a deeper appreciation for the here and now—for ourSELF. We can even appreciate our innocent need for internal or external validation when it arises. These exercises are just a starting point on a journey towards greater self-awareness, healing, feeling, and awakening. Remember, right here, right now, is the only time we truly have, so let's make the most of it by appreciating all that we are and experience.

Dear Friends,

As you reach the final pages of this guide, remember that your journey of healing, feeling, and awakening is always here now. You've taken courageous steps towards uncovering the truth of who you are, and in doing so, you've opened the door to a life of greater freedom, inner peace, and connection. This path is not always easy, but it is profoundly rewarding, and inevitable. Every moment of awareness, every act of kindness, and every step toward self-discovery reveals the boundless love and conscious clarity already within.

You are not alone on this journey. The Collective Healing Anonymous community is here to support you, to walk with you, and to celebrate each victory, no matter how small. Trust in the process, and trust in yourself. Remember that healing is a sacred journey that unfolds in its own time with infinite patience and compassion.

Let this guide and the CHA process be a source of strength and inspiration as you continue to explore, heal, and awaken. You have the power to transform your life, and in doing so, effortlessly inspire others to do the same. You are a beacon of light in this world for simply being, for no reason at all.

You are loved. You ARE love.

Sincerely and Lovingly,

Your CHA Family

unconditional
LOVE

www.ingramcontent.com/pod-product-compliance
Lightning Source LLC
Chambersburg PA
CBHW042141290426
44110CB00002B/75